THE HARVEST HOME

By HANNAH MORE AND OTHERS

Triangle Press
23 5th Ave S. E., Conrad MT 59425
http://www.tripress.com
email: published@tripress.com
406-278-5664 Fax 406-278-5687

ISBN 1-58339-102-9

A Nineteenth Century Story First Published By The American Tract Society

Triangle Press
23 5th Ave S. E., Conrad MT 59425
http://www.tripress.com
email: published@tripress.com
406-278-5664 Fax 406-278-5687

CONTENTS

THE

HARVEST-HOME

HOW quickly does joy often succeed to sorrow, the day of cheerful hope to that of gloomy fear, and the season of plenty and abundance to that of want and scarcity. At one time the dearth of bread in this land was such, that every countenance seemed to gather blackness; the very heavens also appeared to frown upon us; for the weather, during a long time, was so dismal that it threatened to blast the approaching harvest. Having enjoyed many years of plenty without interruption, we had learned to count upon the continuance of the same blessing; and because God's goodness had been so common, we were so much the less thankful for it.

But let us here endeavor to prevent this forgetfulness of our present mercies in the minds of our readers, and let us invite them to come and contemplate with us that greatness and goodness of our Creator, which are so observable at the time of harvest.

There is, indeed, no part of the creation to which we can turn our eyes without meeting with some proofs of the divine power and mercy.

Shall we lift up our eyes to the heavens? There shines the brightness of the sun, which God has placed in the firmament to give light and heat to the world. Shall we wait till the sun is set? Then the moon and the stars take up the same language of praise, and tell of their Maker's power and goodness.

Shall we turn our eyes to the earth? See how the surface of it is spread forth like a carpet, decked with every thing to charm the eye, to delight the sense, and to supply the wants of man. Shall we look upon the great and wide ocean? There go the ships; and behold even the sea is filled with food for the use of man. "How manifold are Thy works, O Lord; in wisdom hast Thou made them all."

The sight of these common objects of nature used often to carry out the holy men of old in praise and adoration to God, of which we will mention an instance in the sixty-fifth Psalm, because it is applicable to the present time—a psalm penned after a long drought, to which had succeeded very plentiful and refreshing rains. The psalmist, while he walks abroad, and delights himself with the beautiful appearance of the harvest, and the prospect of plenty which is on every side, breaks out in the following thanksgiving to the bountiful Giver of all things.

"Praise waiteth for Thee, O God, in Zion; and unto Thee shall the vow be performed. O Thou that hearest prayer, unto Thee shall all flesh come." "Thou makest the outgoings of the morning and evening to rejoice. Thou visitest the earth, and watereth it; Thou greatly enrichest it with the river of God"—for the clouds are compared to a river in the air, sustained by the hand of the Almighty—"Thou preparest corn when Thou hast so provided for it. Thou waterest the ridges thereof abundantly; Thou settlest the furrows thereof; Thou makest it soft with showers; Thou blessest the springing thereof. Thou crownest the year with Thy goodness, and Thy paths drop fatness. The little hills rejoice on every side; the pastures are clothed with flocks; the valleys also are covered over with corn; they shout for joy, they also sing."

To every one who is of the same mind with the psalmist, the same kind of meditations will be very apt to occur. Let us, however, here assist the reader by naming a few subjects, which he will do well to reflect upon while he takes his walk amidst the reapers, and admires the plenty that is in the fields.

First, then, how naturally ought the season of harvest to send our thoughts to the ***great Author*** of it. How clearly is His hand at this time seen. All the power and ingenuity of the whole world cannot frame so much as a single ear of corn. The part which man has in procuring the corn is very small indeed. He in fact does *nothing* himself towards its growth; he only places the seed in a situation which from experience he has found to be favorable to it, and then "he goeth away, and it springeth up he knoweth not how." The seed which he plants was in the first place given by God. When the sower has put it into the ground, there is then a work or operation carried on, in which man is not only unconcerned, but he does not even know how it is accomplished. The grain dies, and from that death a resurrection takes place, a fresh plant arises out of the ground; and this plant is nourished by means of roots hidden within the earth, which then shoot forth without the aid of man. In this secret manner are the different juices collected and sent through the plant; by and by the flower blooms; the ear forms itself, and the corn takes the proper shape and substance; the rain in the meantime waters it, the dews descend, and the sun shines upon it, till at length it is fit for the use of man. In all this, man can do nothing. It is during his absence even that this work is going on. If the grain is blighted, man cannot help it; if it grows too slowly, he is not able to quicken it; he can only look on with hope and fear, and watch it in its different stage; he must ascribe all its growth to the unassisted power of the great Creator of all things.

Plain as the hand of the Creator is in the production of the corn, yet such is our natural ignorance, that while we gather the corn, we often think no more of God in it, than the very cattle which draw it home. The farmer speaks of his own skill, and labor, and pains; and when the grain is ripe, he lays it up in his barn with much self-applause, and begins to count his gains, not considering that all the praise, in fact, is due to God, and that every ear which is laid up is a proof of man's obligation to his Maker.

But let us here notice also the *largeness* of the divine bounty. The works of God are upon a large scale; they are like Himself, infinite. The works of man are little and insignificant; it is but a small spot which his strength can water; but the showers of Heaven water a whole territory at once. It is but a few acres which the diligent labors of man can make productive; but God causes His sun to shine, and his dew to descend, and the whole earth is rendered fruitful. Look over that beautiful and extensive prospect; see as far as the eye can reach how the fields are crowned with plenty; extend the scene in your imagination—still the same rich view of the divine bounty presents itself. Cross the wide ocean, and survey the different countries of which the earth consists. In all the varied productions of these different climates, we only meet with more signs of the divine goodness. How are we then called upon to admire and adore that glorious Being, who suffers no part of the earth to escape His kind and beneficial notice!

With the extensiveness of this bounty, let the *continuance* of it be considered. No sooner is the harvest got in, than again the seed is committed to the ground, and again the same scene returns upon us. Let us carry back our thoughts to the years that have been of old. How unwearied has been our great Benefactor. How unceasing the exertions of His goodness. How many generations have been fed and supported by it. Seasons have changed, but they have only presented different views of the Lord's mercy; and the cold of winter, the bloom of spring, the heat of summer, and the fruits of autumn, have each in its season manifested the same bounty and care of our Creator.

Having indulged in these pleasing reflections upon the divine bounty, it seems proper in the next place to turn our attention to a more melancholy subject—I mean, *our unworthiness of it.* For whom does the Lord open His store, and provide with so liberal a hand? For a race of creatures who are touched with the most lively sense of His goodness, and love and honor Him in proportion to these great obligations?

Do we then hear the reapers, while they cut down the corn, speaking good of the name of the Lord, and blessing Him for His kindness to the children of men? Hark! is it hymns of praise which they are chanting in yonder field? Is the song they sing the song of the psalmist which has just been spoken of? I think, instead of it, some song of profaneness and obscenity is sung aloud. The name of God, indeed, is on many lips, but it is only that it may be trifled with or blasphemed. What, then, are these men gathering God's bounty, and in the same moment profaning His Name? But follow them to the harvest-home; surely now, we may suppose, they meet and offer up their prayer and thanksgiving; and while God is in the act of crowning the year with His bounty, each tongue is loud in talking of His mercy, and each grateful heart is swelling with His praise. But it is commonly reported, that there is no season of the year in which so much wickedness and drunkenness prevail among the farmers, as in that of bringing the harvest home.

Are these, then, the returns which in this year also we are making to the divine goodness? Is all our complaining of want, and our prayer to God for deliverance, to end in a drunken abuse of the mercies He so wonderfully bestows?

But not to dwell on vices which are so great that we would willingly hope they must only be the vices of a few, let us a little consider also the *general* unworthiness of mankind. Who are they that will be fed by this abundant harvest? Will no idle persons be maintained by it? Will no sinners have their strength sustained, so as to continue their life of sin? Will there be none who will eat it with unthankfulness? None who, as the reapers have reaped it without thinking of the Author of the harvest, will in like manner feed upon it without thinking of the Author of their food? Again, will no discontented, murmuring, repining people be fed by the goodness of the Lord? Will all those, in short, whose life is prolonged by the bread now sent them, devote that life to the service of Him who prolonged it?

Surely, if we could remove ourselves to a distance form the earth, and become by any means impartial judges between God and man, we should stand astonished at the present rebellion of the creature. He who made man, He who supports him, sending him the very bread which he eats, has a right to his services, and hath made him, no doubt, for His own glory. I think, if any of us were endowed with power to create some little rational animal inferior to ourselves, and if, after having breathed into him the breath of life, we also daily clothed and nourished him, we should expect his obedience and constant service, in return. And if, after all, such a being should presume to set up for himself, and pretend to have a will of his own, and break all the laws we had given him, we should be ready, I think, to stamp our foot upon him, and to crush him to death at once for not fulfilling the ends of his creation. We should have no patience with such a little insolent and rebellious animal. And yet God has patience with us, notwithstanding all our forgetfulness of the ends for which we were born, and our unthankfulness for the daily returns of His bounty. Nay, though we go on abusing His mercies, He goes on clothing the pastures with His flocks. The valleys also are again covered over with corn; again they shout for joy, they also sing. O let us be ashamed of the baseness of our ingratitude, and repent in the Name of Christ, before the day of His vengeance come upon us.

The season of harvest is also one which should lead us particularly to reflect on our *dependence upon God.* God gave us life at first. He causes our blood to flow, our heart to beat, and our stomach to distribute the nourishment. He too, supplies the food we eat, of whatever kind it be. We may combine together different meats, we may dress them in a variety of ways, but we can create nothing; God is the only Giver of life, and food, and all things; and happy is that man who lives in the lively remembrance of this, who accepts all his comforts as from the hand of the great God—habitually feeling that he has not of himself power to exist for a single moment, or to procure independently of God one single drop of water, or grain of bread. And this sense of our dependence is not a duty only, it is a great comfort also; for how does it tend to relieve all that anxiety which is so natural to us about our existence in the time to come. The more we remember that we are the creatures of God, so much the more shall we trust in Him to provide for His large family, even as a child trusts to the care and prudence of his parent. "Behold the fowls of the air; they sow not, neither do they reap, nor gather into barns, yet your heavenly Father feedeth them."

Next to this sense of our dependence, *gratitude* to God may be mentioned as peculiarly becoming. I think, at this time, not only the heavens above, but the earth beneath, calls aloud upon us to be thankful. Every field, every ear of corn, seems to bid us speak the praises of God. How do these glorify Him, as it were, by an expressive though dumb offering of praise! But man has a tongue with which he can speak forth the praises of his Maker. It is for the sake of man also, that the storehouse of divine bounty is opened; it is for man that the pastures are clothed with flocks, and the valleys covered with corn; it is for man that the sun shines, and the showers descend. From Him, then, should the offering of praise continually ascend.

"But why will you suppose mankind to be so unthankful?" I think I hear some one reply. "Do you think we do not know as well as you that we ought to praise God for a good harvest? There will always, indeed, be a few wicked people in the land, but in general we understand well enough that it is God who sends us bread, and all our mercies; when any of us speak of having a good crop, *Thank God* is the very phrase that is quite common in our lips."

I admit it is so; and I hope, indeed, that many thousand hearts have already offered up the sincere tribute of thanksgiving for the present plentiful season. But we cannot help adding here, that there is a way far beyond that of simple praise, by which true gratitude will manifest itself. It will break out not in words only, but in deeds—in deeds of obedience to Him towards whom the gratitude is felt. What would any father think of the gratitude of a child, or any husband of the gratitude of a wife, which never showed itself in any thing else but a few warm expressions of obligation? No; it is by the readiness and activity in serving the person praised, and by the desire in all respects to please him, that the disposition to gratitude must be judged of. A man may say *thank God* twenty times a day, and yet never truly thank Him in his heart. Words are cheap. Many men think to pay God off, as it were, by this sort of coin.

Let it be remarked, also, that there is a satisfaction and self-complacency which are naturally felt on receiving an abundance of wealth into our lap. We are put into a good humor by it, and when we are reminded that God is the Author of our prosperity, the truth of this is so plain that we cannot deny it; and since our understandings agree to the observation, we fancy that our hearts agree also; whereas, in fact, we only *judge* that God *ought* to be thanked, but we do not thank Him; and as to the good humor we are in, it arises merely from our being well pleased with ourselves, or with the enjoyments which God has given us, and not from out being well pleased with God. That we practice some such frauds as these in ourselves is but too plain; for mark now what follows.

When the same person who has been thanking God so often for His mercies, is by and by called to do something, to suffer something, or to give up something for the sake of serving this gracious Being to whom he professed such great gratitude, he is then either too idle, or too selfish, or too much governed by the opinion of his fellow-creatures, or some way or other too full of excuses to do what is wanted of him. On the other hand, when some temptation comes in his way he yields to it, and sins against the same God as freely as if he were under no obligation to Him. Let us then beware of this hypocritical sort of gratitude, by which we cannot deceive God, though we often delude ourselves by it. Let us show forth His praise not only with our lips, but with our lives. Let us show our sense of His goodness by doing His will, by reading His Word, by attending His worship, by readily denying ourselves for His sake, and in short, by laying out our lives in His service, and by standing forth to promote His cause in a disobedient and unthankful world.

Here let it be hinted, also, that this may be a good time for laying down our plans for using the plenty which is flowing in to us. God has now given us provision for another year, but for what purpose has He given it? In order that we may eat, and drink, and be merry? What, then, have we not immortal souls? The great end of our Creator is, that we may serve Him in this world, and may be prepared to dwell with Him for ever in Heaven. His direction is, that we should employ our health and strength, and all our vigor of body and mind, in fulfilling His will; that we should seek, in the first place, to know God, and Jesus Christ, whom He has sent into the world; and having learned to know Him, that we should then act in our several stations from love to His Name, imitating all His bounty, by ministering to the necessities of our fellow-creatures. Are these then our ends of living? Is this what we propose to ourselves? Are these the views with which we reap the harvest? Are we determined that none of it, as far as in us lies, shall be wasted in riot, or in luxury, or in imprudent consumption? Do we look forward to it as to a treasure, with which the hungry shall be fed, and the poor satisfied? Then, indeed, we may rejoice in the bounty of Heaven, and may reasonably trust that all the expressions of gratitude on our lips are sincere.

Again, let the consideration of the goodness of

God, displayed in the fruits of the earth, raise our minds to the contemplation of those still *greater mercies* which he is able and willing to give us. It is with Him a small matter to provide the earth with food, or to take care of the body. See what rich provision He has made for our souls—for them He has not spared His only begotten Son, but given Him up to be the propitiation for our sins. For the sake of the soul, He has sent His Holy Spirit into the world, to guide men into the knowledge of the truth. For the soul he has prepared an eternal harvest of blessings, "an inheritance which is incorruptible, undefiled, and that fadeth not away, reserved in Heaven for us."

We may learn to value spiritual mercies from what we see of temporal ones. Temporal ones strike the senses, and being suited to our present fallen nature, are more apt to fill our hearts with joy and gratitude. But we may rest assured that the blessings which God hath provided for the soul, are as much superior to those provided for the body, as the soul is to the body, and as eternity is to time. Let us then turn from this earthly scene of abundance to still nobler and larger blessings. Let the fields not only preach to us the immense goodness of our Creator, but let them send our thoughts also to the "unsearchable riches that are in Christ." Let the harvest serve to impress a thoughtless world with wonder, gratitude, reverence, and love to Him who is the Author, not of all our earthly treasures only, but of all the blessings of eternity. In short, let the goodness of God lead us all to repentance, and let each of us take care that the mercies of his Maker be not turned into a curse, by rendering our hearts only so much the more full of this world, and more indifferent to the blessings of the Gospel.

A

HYMN OF PRAISE

FOR

THE ABUNDANT HARVEST OF 1796

AFTER A YEAR OF SCARCITY

Great God, when families threatened late
To scourge our guilty land,
O did we learn from that dark fate,
To dread Thy mighty hand?

Did then our sins to memory rise,
Or owned we God was just?
Or raised we penitential cries,
Or bowed we in the dust?

Did we forsake one evil path;
Was any sin abhorred?
Or did we prevent Thy wrath,
Thus to turn us to the Lord?

'Tis true, we failed not to *repine,*
But did we too *repent,*
Or own the chastisement divine,
In awful judgment sent?

Though the bright chain of peace is broke,
And war with ruthless sword
Unpeoples nations at a stroke,
Yet who regards the Lord?

But God, who in His strict decrees
Remembers mercy still,
Can in a moment, if He please,
Our hearts with comfort fill.

He marked our angry spirits rise,
Domestic hate increase,
And for a time withheld supplies,
To teach us love and peace.

He, when He brings His children low,
Has blessings still in store;
And when He strikes the heaviest blow,
He does but love us more.

Now frost, and flood, and blight no more
Our golden harvests spoil,
See what an unexampled store
Rewards the reapers' toil.

HYMN OF PRAISE

As when the promised harvest failed
In Canaan's fruitful land,
The envious patriarchs were assailed
By famine's pressing hand,

The angry brothers then forgot
Each fierce and jarring feud;
United by their adverse lot,
They loved as brothers should.

So here, from Heaven's correcting hand,
Though famine failed to move,
Let plenty now throughout the land
Rekindle peace and love.

Like the rich fool, let us not say,
Soul, thou hast goods in store;
But shake the overplus away,
To feed the aged poor.

Let rich and poor, on whom are now
Such bounteous crops bestowed,
Raise many a pure and holy vow
In gratitude to God.

And while His gracious Name we praise,
For bread so kindly given,
Let us beseech Him all our days,
To give the Bread of Heaven.

In that blest prayer our Lord did frame,
Of all our prayers the guide,
We ask that "hallowed be *His* Name,"
And then our needs supplied.

For grace He bids us first implore,
Next, that we may be fed;
We say, "Thy will be done," before
We ask "our daily bread."
We ask "our daily bread."

THE

PILGRIMS

AN ALLEGORY

BY HANNAH MORE

I THOUGHT I was once upon a time travelling through a certain land which was very full of people; but what was rather odd, not one of all this multitude was at home—they were all bound to a far distant country. Though it was permitted by the Lord of the land that these pilgrims might associate together for their present mutual comfort and convenience, and each was not only allowed, but commanded to do the others all the services he could upon their journey, yet it was decreed, that every individual traveller must enter the far country singly.

There was a great gulf at the end of the journey, which every one must pass along and at his own risk, and the friendship of the whole united world could be of no use in passing that gulf. The exact time when each was to pass was not known to any; this the Lord always kept a close secret out of kindness; yet still they were as sure that the time must come, and that at no very great distance, as if they had been informed of the very moment. Now, as they knew they were always liable to be called away at an hour's notice, one would have thought they would have been chiefly employed in packing up, and preparing, and getting every thing in order. But this was so far from being the case, that it was almost the only thing they did not think about.

Now I only appeal to you, my readers, if any of you are setting out upon a little common journey, if it is only to London or York, is not all your leisure time employed in settling your business at home and packing up every little necessity for your expedition? And does not the fear of neglecting any thing you ought to remember, or may have occasion for, haunt your mind, and sometimes even intrude upon you unseasonably? And when you are actually on your journey, especially if you have never been to that place before, or are likely to remain there, don't you begin to think a little about the pleasures and the employments of the place, and to wish to know a little what sort of a city London or York is?

Don't you wonder what is doing there, and whether you are properly qualified for the business or the company you expect to be engaged in? Do you never look at the map? And don't you try to pick up from your fellow-passengers in the stage-coach any little information you can get? And though you may be obliged, out of civility, to converse with them on common subjects, yet do not your secret thoughts still run upon London or York, its business, or its pleasures? And, above all, if you are likely to set out early, are you not afraid of oversleeping, and does not that fear keep you upon the watch, so that you are commonly up and ready before the porter comes to summon you? Reader, if this be your case, how surprised will you be to hear, that the travellers to the far country have not half your prudence, though bound on a journey of infinitely more importance, to a land where nothing can be sent after them, and in which, when they are once settled, all errors are not recoverable.

I observed that these pilgrims, instead of being upon the watch, lest they should be ordered off unprepared—instead of laying up any provision, or even making memorandums of what they would be likely to want, spend most of their time in crowds, either in the way of traffic or diversions. At first, when I saw them so much engaged in conversing with each other, I thought it a good sign, and listened attentively to their talk, not doubting but the chief turn of it would be about the climate, or treasures, or society they should probably meet with in the far country. I supposed they might be also discussing about the best and safest road to it, and that each was availing himself of the knowledge of his neighbor, on a subject of equal importance to all. I listened to every party, but in scarcely any did I hear one word about the land to which they were bound, though it was their home, the place where their whole interest, expectation, and inheritance lay; to which also great part of their friends had gone before, and whither they were sure all the rest would follow.

Instead of this, their whole talk was about the business, or the pleasures, or the fashions of the strange country which they were merely passing through, and in which they had not one foot of land which they were sure of calling their own for the next quarter of an hour. What little estate they had was *personal* and not real, and that was a mortgaged life-hold dwelling of clay, not properly their own, but only lent to them on a short, uncertain lease, of which seventy years was considered as the longest period, and very few indeed lived in it to the end of the term; for this was always at the *will of the Lord,* part of whose choice it was, that He could take away the lease at pleasure, knock down the stoutest inhabitant at a single blow, and turn out the poor shivering, helpless tenant naked, to that far country for which he had made no provision.

Sometimes, in order to quicken the pilgrim in

his preparation, the Lord would break down the dwelling by slow degrees—sometimes he would let it tumble by its own natural decay; for as it was only built to last a certain term, it would sometimes grow so uncomfortable by increasing wear, even before the ordinary lease was out, that the lodging was hardly worth keeping, though the tenant could seldom be persuaded to think so, but fondly clung to it to the last. First the thatch on the top of the dwelling changed color, then it fell off, and left the roof bare; then "the grinders ceased because they were few;" then the windows became so darkened that the owner could scarcely see through them; then one prop fell away, then another, then the supports became bent, and the whole fabric trembled and tottered, with every other symptom of a falling house.

On some occasions, the Lord ordered His messengers, of which he had a great variety, to batter, injure, deface, and almost abolish the frail building, even while it seemed new and strong; this was what the Landlord called *giving warning;* but many a tenant would not take warning, and was so fond of staying where he was, even under all these inconveniences, that at last he was cast out by ejection, not being prevailed on to leave his dwelling in a proper manner, though one would have thought the fear of being turned out would have whetted his diligence in preparing for "a better and a more enduring inheritance."

For though the people were only tenants at will in these crazy dwellings, yet, through the goodness of the same Lord, they were assured that He never turned them out of these habitations before He had on His part provided for them a better, so that there was not such another Landlord in the world; and though their present dwelling was but frail, being only slightly equipped to serve the occasion, yet they might hold their future possession by a most certain position, the Word of the Lord Himself, which was entered in a covenant, or title-deed, consisting of many sheets; and because a great many good things were given away in this deed, a book was made of which every soul might get a copy.

This indeed had not always been the case, because, till a few ages back, there had been a sort of monopoly in the case, and "the wise and prudent," that is, the cunning and fraudful, had hid these things from the "babes and sucklings," that is, from the low and ignorant, and many frauds had been practiced, and the poor had been cheated of their right; so that not being allowed to read and judge for themselves, they had been sadly imposed upon; but all these tricks had been put an end to more than two hundred years when I passed through the country, and the meanest man who could read might then have a copy, so that he might see himself what he had to trust to; and even those who could not read might hear it read once or twice every week at least, without pay, by learned men, whose business it was.

But it surprised me to see how few comparatively made use of these vast advantages. Of those who *had* a copy, many laid it carelessly by, expressed a *general* belief in the truth of the title-deed, a *general* satisfaction that they should come in for a share of the inheritance, a *general* good opinion of the Lord whose Word it was, and a *general* disposition to take His promise upon trust; always, however, intending, at a "convenient season," to inquire further into the matter; but this convenient season seldom came, and this neglect of theirs was translated by their Lord into the forfeiture of the inheritance.

At the end of this country lay the vast gulf mentioned before; it was shadowed over by a broad and thick cloud, which prevented the pilgrims from seeing in a distinct manner what was doing behind it, yet such beams of brightness now and then darted through the cloud as enabled those who used a telescope provided for that purpose, to see "the substance of things hoped for;" but it was not every one who could make use of this telescope; no eye indeed was *naturally* disposed to it; but an earnest desire of getting a glimpse of the invisible realities, gave such a strength and steadiness to the eye which used the telescope, as enabled it to see many things which could not be seen by the natural sight. Above the cloud was this inscription: "The things which are seen are temporal; but the things which are not seen are eternal." Of these last things many glorious descriptions had been given; but as those splendors were at a distance, and as the pilgrims in general did not care to use the telescope, these distant glories made little impression.

The glorious inheritance which lay beyond the cloud, was called "the things above;" while a multitude of insignificant objects, which appeared contemptibly small when looked at through the telescope, were called "the things below." Now, as we know it is nearness which gives size and bulk to any object, it was not surprising that these ill-judging pilgrims were more struck with these trinkets and trifles, which by lying close at hand were visible and tempting to the naked eye, and which made up the sum of "the things below," than with the remote glories of "the things above;" but this was chiefly owing to their not making use of the telescope, through which, if you examined thoroughly "the things below," they seemed to shrink almost down to nothing, which was indeed their real size; while "the things above" appeared the more beautiful and vast, the more the telescope was used.

But the surprising part of the story was this, not that the pilgrims were captivated at first sight with "the things below," for that was natural enough; but that, when they had tried them all over and over, and found themselves deceived and disappointed in almost every one of them, it did not at all lessen their fondness, and they grasped at them again with the same eagerness as before. There were some gay fruits which looked alluring, but on being opened, instead of a kernel, they were found to contain rottenness, and those which seemed the fullest often proved on trial to be quite hollow and empty. Those which were most tempting to the eye were often found to be wormwood to the taste, or poison to the stomach; and many flowers that seemed most bright and gay, had a worm gnawing at the root.

Among the chief attractions of "the things

below," were certain little lumps of yellow clay, on which almost every eye and every heart was fixed. When I saw the variety of uses to which this clay could be converted, and the respect which was shown to those who could scrape together the greatest number of pieces, I did not much wonder at the general desire to pick up some of them. But when I beheld the anxiety, the wakefulness, the competitions, the tricks, the frauds, the scuffling, the pushing, the turmoiling, the kicking, the shoving, the cheating, the scheming, the envy, the malignity, which were excited by a desire to possess this article—when I saw the general scramble among those who had little to get much, and of those who had much to get more, then I could not help applying to these people a proverb in use among us, that "gold may be bought too dear."

Though I saw that there were various sorts of trinkets which engaged the hearts of different travellers, such as a measure of red or blue ribbon, for which some were content to forfeit their future inheritance, committing the sin of Esau without his temptation of hunger; yet the yellow clay I found was the grand object for which most hands were scrambling and most souls were risked. One thing was extraordinary, that the nearer these people were to being turned

out of their dwelling, the fonder they grew of these pieces of clay; so that I naturally concluded they meant to take the clay with them to the far country, to assist them in their establishment in it; but I soon learned this clay was not useful there, the Lord having declared to these pilgrims, that as they had "brought nothing into this world, they could carry nothing out."

I inquired of the different people who were raising the various heaps of clay, some of a larger, some of a smaller size, why they discovered such unceasing anxiety, and for whom. Some, whose piles were immense, told me they were heaping up for their children; this I thought very right, till on casting my eyes round, I observed many of the children of those very people had large heaps of their own. Others told me it was for their grandchildren; but on inquiry I found these were not yet born, and in many cases there was little chance that they ever would be. The truth, on a close examination, proved to be, that the true genuine heapers really heaped for themselves—that it was in fact neither for friend nor child, but to gratify an inordinate appetite of their own. Nor was I much surprised after this to see these yellow hoards at length, "canker, and the rust of them became a witness" against the hoarders, and "eat their flesh as it were fire."

Many, however, who had set out with a high heap of their father's raising, before they had got one-third of their journey, had scarcely a single piece left. As I was wondering what had caused these enormous piles to vanish in so short a time, I beheld scattered up and down the country all sorts of odd inventions, for some or other of which the vain possessors of the great heaps of clay had traded and bartered them away in fewer hours than their ancestors had spent years in getting them together. O, what a strange unaccountable medley it was; and what was ridiculous enough, I observed that the greatest quantity of the clay was always exchanged for things that were of no use that I could discover, owing, I suppose, to my ignorance of the manners of that country.

In one place I saw large heaps exhausted in order to set two idle, pampered horses to running; but the worst part of the joke was, the horses did not run to fetch or carry any thing, but merely to let the gazers see which could run fastest. Now this gift of swiftness exercised to no one useful purpose, was only one out of many instances I observed of talent employed to no end.

In another place I saw whole piles of the clay spent to maintain long ranges of buildings full of dogs, on provisions which would have supplied some thousands of pilgrims who were sadly in need, and whose ragged dwellings were exhausted for want of a little help to repair them. Some of the piles were regularly pulled down once in seven years, in order to corrupt certain needy pilgrims to belie their consciences.

Others were spent in playing with white stiff bits of paper painted over with red and black spots, in which I thought there must be some trickery, because the very touch of these painted pasteboards made the heaps fly from one to another, and back again to the same, in a way that natural causes could not account for. There was another proof that there must be some magic in this business, which was, that if a pasteboard with red spots fell into a hand which wanted a black one, the person changed color, his eyes flashed fire, and he discovered other symptoms of madness, which showed there was some witchcraft in the case. These clean little pasteboards, as harmless as they looked, had the wonderful power of pulling down the highest piles in less time than all the other causes put together. I observed that many small piles were given in exchange for an enchanted liquor, which when the purchaser had drank to a little excess, he lost all power of managing the rest of his heap, without losing the love of it.

Now I found it was the opinion of sober pilgrims, that either hoarding the clay, or trading it for any such purposes as the above, was thought exactly the same offense in the eyes of the Lord; and it was expected that when they should come under His more immediate jurisdiction in "the far country," the penalty fixed to hoarding and squandering would be nearly the same. While I examined the countenances of the owners of the heaps, I observed that those who I well knew never intended to make any use at all of their heap, were far more terrified at the thought of losing it, or of being torn from it, than those who were employing it in the most useful manner. Those who best knew what to do with it, set their hearts least upon it, and were always most willing to leave it. But such riddles were common in this odd country. It was indeed a very land of paradox.

Now I wondered why these pilgrims, who were naturally made erect, with an eye formed to look up to "the things above," yet had their eyes almost constantly bent in the other direction, riveted to the earth, and fastened "on things below," just like those animals who walk on all-fours. I was told they had not always been subject to this weakness of sight and proneness on earth—that they had originally been upright and beautiful, having been created after the image of the Lord, and that He had placed them in a superior habitation, which He had given them years ago; but that their first ancestors fell from it through pride and disobedience—that upon this, the inheritance was taken away, they lost their original strength, brightness and beauty, became as dead, and were driven into this strange country; where, *however,* the Lord showed them mercy and restored life through His Son; and His likeness; for they had become disfigured, and had grown so unlike Him, that you would hardly believe they were His own children, though, in some, the resemblances had become again visible.

The Lord, however, was so merciful, that instead of giving them up to the dreadful consequence of their own folly, as He might have done witout any impeachment of His justice, He gave them immediate comfort, and promised them that in due time His own Son should come down and restore them to the future inheritance which He should purchase for them. And now it was, that in order to keep up their spirits, after they had lost their estate through the folly of their ancestors, that He began to give them a part of their former title-deed. He continued to send them portions of it from time to time by different faithful servants, whom, however, these ungrateful people generally used ill, and some of whom they murdered.

But for all this the Lord was so very forgiving, that He at length sent these rebellious ones a proclamation of full and free pardon by His Son, who, though they used Him in a more cruel manner than they had done any of His servants, yet after having "finished the work His Father had given Him to do," went back into "the far country," to prepare a place for all them who believe in Him; and there He still lives, pleading for those he still loves and forgives, and will restore to the purchased inheritance on the terms of their being heartily sorry for what they have done, thoroughly desirous of pardon, and convinced that He is able and willing to "save to the uttermost all them that come unto God by Him."

I saw, indeed, that many old offenders appeared to be sorry for what they had done; that is, they did not like to be punished for it. They were willing enough to be delivered from the penalty of their sin, but they did not heartily wish to be delivered from the power of it. Many declared, in the most public manner, once every week, that they were very sorry they had done amiss—that they had "erred and strayed like lost SHEEP;' but it was not enough to *declare* their sorrow ever so often, if they gave no other sign of their penitence. For there was so little truth in them, that the Lord required other proofs of their sincerity besides their own word, for they often lied with their lips and dissembled with their tongue. But those who professed to be penitents were neither allowed to raise heaps of clay, by circumventing their neighbors, or to keep great piles lying by them useless; nor must they barter them for any of those idle vanities which reduced the heaps on a sudden; for I found that among the grand articles of future reckoning, the use they had made of the heaps would be a principal one.

I was sorry to observe many of the fairer part of these pilgrims spend too much of their heaps in adorning and beautifying their dwellings of clay, in painting, whitewashing, and enamelling them. All these tricks, however, did not preserve them from decay, and when they grew old, they even looked worse for all this cost and varnish. Some, however, acted a more sensible part, and spent no more upon their mouldering dwellings than just to keep them whole and clean, and in good repair, which is what every tenant ought to do; and I observed that those who were most moderate in their care of their own dwellings, were most attentive to repair and warm the ragged dwellings of others. But none did this with much zeal or acceptance but those who had acquired a habit of overlooking "the things below," and who also, by the constant use of the telescope, had got their natural weak and dim sight so strengthened as to be able to discern pretty distinctly the nature of "the things above." The habit of fixing their eyes on these glories made all the shining trifles which compose the mass of "things below," at last appear in their own smallness. For it was in this case particularly true, that things are only big or little by comparison; and there was no other way of making "the things below" appear as small as they really were, but by comparing them, by means of the telescope, with "the things above." But I observed that the false judgment of the pilgrims ever kept pace with their wrong practices; for those who kept their eyes fastened on "the things below," were reckoned wise in their generation, while the few who looked forward to the future glories, were accounted by the bustlers, or heapers, to be either fools or mad.

Most of these pilgrims went on in adorning their dwellings, adding to their heaps, grasping "the things below" as if they would never let them go, shutting their eyes instead of using their telescope, and neglecting their title-deed as if it was the parchment of another man's estate, and not of their own, till, one after another, each felt his dwelling tumbling about his ears.

Oh then what a busy, bustling, anxious terrifying, distracting moment was that! What a deal of business was to be done, and what a strange time was this to do it in! Now to see the confusion and dismay, occasioned by having left every thing to the last minute. First some one was sent for to make over the yellow heaps to another, which the heaper now found would be of no use to himself in crossing the gulf—a transfer which ought to have been made while the dwelling was sound.

Then there was a consultation between two or three masons at once, perhaps to try to patch up the walls, and strengthen the props, and stop the decay of the tumbling dwelling; but not till the masons were forced to declare it was past repairing—a truth they were rather too willing to keep back—did the tenant seriously think it was time to pack up, prepare, and be gone.

Then what sending for the wise men who professed to explain the title-deed; and Oh, what remorse that they had neglected to examine it till their senses were too confused for so weighty a business! What reproaches, or what exhortations to others to look better after their own affairs than they had done! Even to the wisest of the inhabitants the falling of their dwelling was a solemn thing—solemn, but nor surprising; they had long been packing up and preparing; they praised their Lord's goodness that they had been allowed to stay so long; many acknowledged the mercy of their frequent warnings, and confessed that those very dilapidations which had made the house uncomfortable had been a blessing, as it had set them on diligent preparation for their future inheritance, had made them more earnest in examining their title to it, and had set them on such a frequent application to the telescope, that "the things above" had seemed every day to approach nearer and nearer, and "the things below" to recede and vanish in proportion. These desired not to be "unclothed, but to be clothed upon;" for they knew "that if the earthly house of this tabernacle was dissolved, they had a house not made with hands, eternal in the heavens."

TURN THE CARPET

OR

THE TWO WEAVERS

IN

A DIALOGUE BETWEEN DICK AND JOHN

BY HANNAH MORE

As at their work two weavers sat,
Passing time with friendly chat,
They touched upon the price of meat,
So high a weaver scarce could eat.

"What with my children and sickly wife,"
Quoth Dick, "I'm almost tired of life;
So hard my work, so poor my fare,
'Tis more than mortal man can bear.

"How glorious is the rich man's state,
His house so fine, his wealth so great;
Heaven is unjust, you must agree;
Why all to him? Why none to me?

"In spite of what the Scripture teaches,
In spite of all the parson preaches,
This worl—indeed I've thought so long—
Is ruled, I think, extremely wrong.

"Wherever I look, however I range,
'Tis all confused, and hard, and strange;
The good are troubled and oppressed,
And all the wicked are the blessed."

Quoth John, "Our ignorance is the cause
Why thus we blame our Maker's laws;
Part of His ways alone we know,
'Tis all that man can see below.

"Seest thou that carpet, not half done,
Which thou, dear Dick, has well begun?
Behold the wild confusion there;
So rude the mass it makes one stare.

"A stranger, ignorant of the trade,
Would say, 'No meaning's there conveyed;
For where's the middle—where's the border?
Thy carpet now is all disorder.'"

Quoth Dick, "My work is yet in bits,
But still in every part it fits;
Besides, you reason like a lout;
Why, man, *that carpet's inside out.*"

Says John, "Thou sayest the thing I mean,
And now I hope to cure thy spleen;
This world, which clouds thy soul with doubt,
Is but a carpet inside out.

"As when we view these shreds and ends,
We know not what the whole intends;
So, when on earth things look but odd,
They're working still some scheme of God.

"No plan, no pattern can we trace—
All wants proportion, truth, and grace;
The motley mixture we deride,
Nor see the beauteous upper side.

"But when we reach the world of light,
And view those works of God aright,
Then shall we see the whole design,
And own the Workman is divine.

"What now seem random strokes, will there
All order and design appear;
Then shall we praise what here we spurned,
For then the *carpet shall be turned.*"
Thou art right," quoth Dick; "no more I'll grumble,
That this world is so strange a jumble;
My impious doubts are put to flight,
For my own carpet sets me right."